WRITING FRAMEWORKS

A THEMATIC APPROACH

Recount

Exposition

Report

Narrative

Explanation

Description

Procedure

Rosalba Bottega & Yolande Colwell

PR–0267

ISBN 1-86400-624-2

9 781864 006247

Prim-Ed Publishing

www.prim-ed.com

Writing Frameworks—Middle
Prim-Ed Publishing

First published in 2000 by R.I.C. Publications
Reprinted under license in 2000 by Prim-Ed Publishing

ISBN 1 86400 624 2
PR–0267

Additional titles available in this series:
Writing Frameworks—Lower
Writing Frameworks—Upper

Home Page: http://www.prim-ed.com

Prim-Ed Publishing Pty. Ltd.
Offices in: United Kingdom: PO Box 051, Nuneaton, Warwickshire, CV11 6ZU   **Email:** sales@prim-ed.com
               Australia: PO Box 332, Greenwood, Western Australia, 6924   **Email:** ozsales@prim-ed.com
               Republic of Ireland: PO Box 8, New Ross, County Wexford, Ireland   **Email:** sales@prim-ed.iol.ie

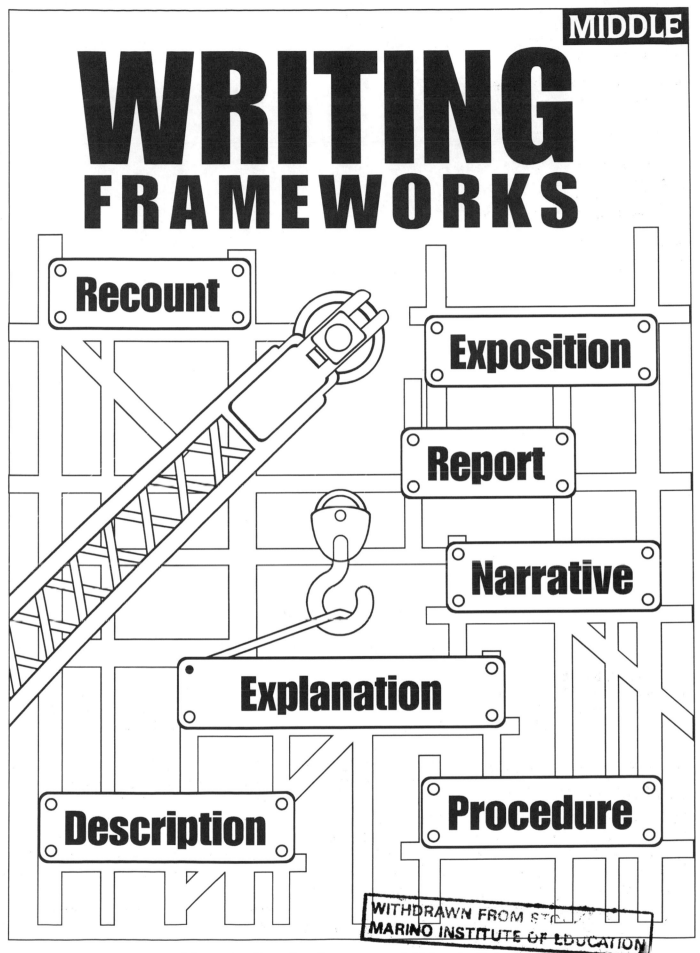

MIDDLE

WRITING
FRAMEWORKS

Recount

Exposition

Report

Narrative

Explanation

Description

Procedure

Written by Rosalba Bottega and Yolande Colwell

Published by Prim-Ed Publishing
www.prim-ed.com

Foreword

Writing Frameworks – Middle is one in a series of three photocopiable resources designed to familiarise pupils with writing frameworks through a thematic approach.

Each framework (recount, narrative, description, report, procedure, explanation and exposition) is based on a different theme and written in a clear step-by-step format. A collection of support activities follows each framework. These activities range from:

- writing individual texts in the given framework outline
- comprehension questions
- a variety of word study activities
- cloze

Assessment examples and answers are also provided for teacher use, and a writing checklist is provided for pupil self-assessment.

The final section in this book is a learning centre to be used by independent pupils or as directed by the teacher. It consists of writing and creative activities. Teachers may choose to make these activities into individual work cards or simply enlarge the worksheet and allow pupils to choose an activity. A pupil response sheet has been provided for each activity.

Other books in this series are:

Writing Frameworks – Lower
Writing Frameworks – Upper

Contents

Curriculum Links

The English Language Revised Primary School Curriculum for Ireland encourages children to write using a wide range of genres. It also encourages the integration of oral language, reading and writing in a coherent language process. Both of these characteristics have been taken into consideration in *Writing Frameworks*, which is a series of three books featuring a variety of themed frameworks for writing. The series also contains a variety of comprehension and word study activities. *Writing Frameworks* covers many of the content objectives from the strands of the English Language curriculum. They include that the child should be enabled to:

Book	Strand	Strand Unit	Class	Content Objectives
Lower	Receptiveness to language	Writing	1st & 2nd	• Experience a classroom environment that encourages writing • Observe the teacher as he/she models writing • Seek help from the teacher in order to achieve accuracy and an appropriate standard of presentation • Experience how story structure is organised by reading and listening to fiction • Explore different genres • Have writing valued
	Competence and confidence in using language	Writing	1st & 2nd	• Realise that first attempts at writing are not necessarily the finished product and learn to undertake second drafts in order to improve writing • Have regular opportunities to write for himself/herself or for others
	Developing cognitive abilities through language	Writing	1st & 2nd	• Write in a variety of genres • Write the significant details about an event or an activity • Write an explanation for something
	Emotional and imaginative development through language	Writing	1st & 2nd	• Write about experiences • Draw and write stories and poems
Middle	Receptiveness to language	Writing	3rd & 4th	• Experience a classroom environment that encourages writing • Observe the teacher modelling different writing genres • Write stories that explore a variety of genres • See his/her writing valued
	Competence and confidence in using language	Writing	3rd & 4th	• Write regularly, and gradually extend the period over which a writing effort is sustained • Learn to use questions as a mechanism for expanding and developing a story • Give sequence to ideas and events in stories • Develop an appreciation of how the intended audience should influence the nature of a piece of writing • Learn to revise and re-draft writing

Curriculum Links

Book	Strand	Strand Unit	Class	Content Objectives
Middle	Developing cognitive abilities through language	Writing	3rd & 4th	• Write in a variety of genres with greater sophistication • Write about ideas encountered in other areas of the curriculum • Write down directions on how to perform a particular process • Expand and clarify his/her thoughts on a particular idea or topic through drafting and re-drafting
	Emotional and imaginative development through language	Writing	3rd & 4th	• Express his/her reactions to particular experiences in writing • Create stories
Upper	Receptiveness to language	Writing	5th & 6th	• Experience a classroom environment that encourages writing • Observe the teacher model a wide variety of writing genres • Experience interesting and relevant writing challenges • Receive and give constructive responses to writing • See his/her writing valued • Experience a level of success in writing that will be an incentive to continue writing
	Competence and confidence in using language	Writing	5th & 6th	• Write regularly • Write for a sustained length of time • Write independently through a process of drafting, revising, editing and publishing • Choose a register of language appropriate to subject and audience • Choose a form and quality of presentation appropriate to the audience
	Developing cognitive abilities through language	Writing	5th & 6th	• Write in a wide variety of genres • Write for a particular purpose and with a particular audience in mind • Refine ideas and their expression through drafting and re-drafting • Argue the case in writing for a particular point of view
	Emotional and imaginative development through language	Writing	5th & 6th	• Write stories and poems

Assessment Sheet

Pupil Name	Recount		Narrative		Description		Report		Procedure		Explanation		Exposition	
	Dev.	Mast.	Dev.	Mast.	Dev.	Mast.	Dev.	Mast.	Dev.	Mast.	Dev.	Mast.	Dev.	Mast.
Comment														
Comment														
Comment														
Comment														
Comment														
Comment														
Comment														
Comment														
Comment														
Comment														
Comment														
Comment														
Comment														

Dev. = Developing   Mast. = Mastered

Writing Checklist

Colour the face to show how you think
you are going with your writing.

I followed the framework.	😠	😐	🙂
My writing makes sense.	😠	😐	🙂
I have correctly used all the punctuation required.	😠	😐	🙂
I have written a topic sentence with related information in the correct paragraph form.	😠	😐	🙂
My writing is very descriptive.	😠	😐	🙂

- -

Writing Checklist

Colour the face to show how you think
you are going with your writing.

I followed the framework.	😠	😐	🙂
My writing makes sense.	😠	😐	🙂
I have correctly used all the punctuation required.	😠	😐	🙂
I have written a topic sentence with related information in the correct paragraph form.	😠	😐	🙂
My writing is very descriptive.	😠	😐	🙂

The World Cup Football Finals

A recount is a framework that retells events as they happened in time order.
Examples of this type of writing include personal experiences, journals, autobiograpies, diary writing, history books and eyewitness accounts.

Opening Statement (Who, when, what, where and why)

Last Friday was a miserable day. The rain was pounding and the wind's strong howl frightened me. As I looked out of my window all I could see were dark clouds. The weather concerned me as Dad and I were going to the football on Saturday to watch the World Cup finals. Dad had won tickets through his work and had decided to take me as his buddy. It was an event I was looking forward to for a long time. Dad had been a player for his town's football team in his younger years and it was my dream to follow in his footsteps.

Event One (Events in time order)

Fortunately, the weather turned on Saturday. The sun was shining brightly and the dark clouds were no longer to be seen. The rain had ceased and the grounds were drying. We packed our lunch and set off for the match. Both Dad and I were bursting with excitement.

Event Two

Throughout the game I could feel a build-up of tension among the spectators. Italy and Brazil were not the teams I barracked for but their amazing skills and excellent display of teamwork had me staring at the players. I could not take my eyes off them.

Event Three

The final ten minutes was the most awesome display of football I had ever witnessed. On an equal score of one all, the teams were given extra time. As Italy headed for their goals Brazil's keeper failed to block the most spectacular goal. Italy's supporters clambered to their feet roaring and cheering.

Conclusion (Ending Statement)

Italy had won the cup. Despite their loss, Brazil's captain congratulated the Italian team in an honourable manner. He was definitely a good sport. Dad and I had the most fantastic day.

The World Cup Football Finals

Use the recount to answer the questions.

1. Why was Friday's weather a concern to the author?

2. What do the terms 'the weather turned' refer to?

3. Was the game in the morning, afternoon or evening? How do you know?

4. Which part of the game was the most exciting? Why?

5. Why couldn't the author take his eyes off the teams?

6. Do you agree with the author in saying that Brazil's captain was a 'good sport?'

   _____ Why? _____

7. How would you describe someone who is a 'good sport'? Give a real-life example.

8. Draw Italy kicking the winning goal.

The World Cup Football Finals

Last Friday was a miserable day. The rain was pounding and the _____(1) strong howl frightened me. As I looked out of my window all I could see were dark clouds.

The _____(2) concerned me as Dad and I were going to the football on Saturday to watch the World Cup finals. Dad had won tickets through his work and had decided to take me as his _____(3). It was an event I was looking forward to for a long time. Dad had been a player for his town's football _____(4) in his younger years and it was my dream to follow in his footsteps.

Fortunately, the weather turned on Saturday. The sun _____(5) shining brightly and the dark _____(6) were no longer to be seen. The rain had ceased and the grounds were drying. We packed our _____(7) and set off for the match. Both Dad and I were _____(8) with excitement.

Throughout the game I could feel a build-up of _____(9) among the spectators. Italy and Brazil were not the teams I barracked for _____(10) their amazing skills _____(11) excellent display of teamwork had me staring at the players. I could not take my eyes off them.

The _____(12) ten minutes was the most awesome display of football I had ever witnessed. On an equal score of one all, the teams were given _____(13) time. As _____(14) headed for their goals Brazil's keeper failed to block the most spectacular goal. Italy's supporters clambered to _____(15) feet roaring and cheering.

Italy had won the cup. Despite their _____,(16) Brazil's captain congratulated the Italian _____(17) in an honourable manner. He was definitely a good _____(18). Dad and I had the most fantastic day.

The World Cup Football Finals

1. Antonyms

An antonym is a word that is the opposite to another. For example, hot and cold.

Study the words below. Find eight pairs of antonyms and list them.

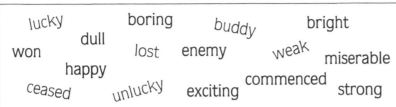

lucky   boring   buddy   bright
won   dull   lost   enemy   weak   miserable
happy   commenced
ceased   unlucky   exciting   strong

_____ , _____   _____ , _____

_____ , _____   _____ , _____

_____ , _____   _____ , _____

_____ , _____   _____ , _____

2. Synonyms

**A synonym is a word that has a similar meaning to another.
For example, horrible and awful.**

Study the words below. Find eight pairs of synonyms and list them.

fortunately   stopped   tough   great
looking   strong   score   luckily   ceased   extra
results   wonderful   see   staring   more   witness

_____ , _____   _____ , _____

_____ , _____   _____ , _____

_____ , _____   _____ , _____

_____ , _____   _____ , _____

3.

Use some of the antonyms and synonyms above in a nonsense paragraph. Underline the antonyms and synonyms. Illustrate your paragraph.

The World Cup Football Finals

1. Rewrite the following words in alphabetical order.

   (a)   tickets, miserable, weather, Saturday, game

   _____

   (b)   buddy, brightly, barracked, ceased, decided

   _____

   (c)   equal, Italy, clambered, captain, honourable

   _____

   (d)   won, window, wind, world, witnessed

   _____

2. Study the words below and write the word from the brackets that comes alphabetically before the word in bold print.

   (a)   (fun, feet, frog) **football**   _____

   (b)   (product, proven, packed) **proceeded**   _____

   (c)   (dad, did, display) **decided**   _____

3. Use a dictionary to find two words that come between the pairs of words below.

   (a)   ground   growing   _____   _____

   (b)   dismay   display   _____   _____

   (c)   mistake   mister   _____   _____

4. Write the meaning of the following words and list the dictionary page number.

Word	Meaning	Page
awesome		
pounding		
miserable		

Writing a Recount

Write a recount that tells a story about something that you have been to. Follow the layout below.

Title: _____

Opening Statement (When, who, what, where and why?)

_____

_____

_____

_____

Event 1

_____

_____

_____

_____

Event 2

_____

_____

_____

_____

Event 3

_____

_____

_____

_____

Ending (Concluding Statement)

_____

_____

_____

_____

Edit and publish your recount on another piece of paper. Illustrate your recount.

The Fox and the Crow

A narrative is a framework that tells a story. It has a plot, with a complication and resolution.

Examples of this type of writing include fairytales, novels, myths, legends, fables, fantasy and poems.

Setting (When, who, where?)

One day a crow stole a piece of cheese. He flew to a nearby tree with the cheese as he thought that it would be a great place to eat it.

Initiating Event (What starts the story?)

A fox spied the crow and the cheese. He thought to himself that the cheese would be delicious to eat.

Problem
(What makes the story exciting?)

With this in mind, he devised a plan to get the cheese from the crow. The fox said to the crow, 'You are beautiful. I have never before set eyes upon such a shiny coat and sparkling eyes!'. The crow was very pleased.

The fox then said to the crow, 'Since you look so magnificent I'm sure that your voice would also be of the same quality!'.

Resolution
(How is the problem solved?)

The flattery certainly made the crow feel very happy. In fact, it made her want to demonstrate to the fox how magnificent her voice was. She opened up her mouth wide and the cheese fell to the ground. Quickly the fox ran towards the cheese and picked it up.

Conclusion (How does the story end?)

To the crow he said, 'You may sing like an angel and look wonderful, however, you are not very clever!'. With that, the fox ran away. The crow thought to herself that next time she would not be so easily fooled.

Moral: Beware of flatterers. They are not to be trusted.

The Fox and the Crow

Use the fable to answer the questions.

1. Where do you think the fable was set? Why?

_____

_____

_____

2. Who do you think the crow stole the cheese from? Why?

_____

_____

3. Explain the meaning of these words.

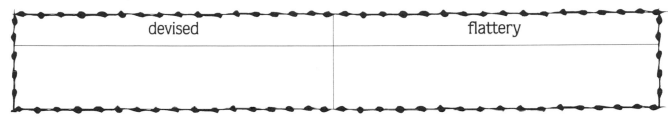

devised	flattery

4. How did the fox get the crow to open her mouth?

_____

_____

5. What is another way the fox could have made the crow open her mouth?

_____

_____

6. How did the crow feel when the fox ran away with the cheese?

_____

_____

7. (a) Explain the moral of the story.

_____

_____

_____

_____

(b) Write a different title for the fable.

_____

_____

_____

_____

The Fox and the Crow

One day a crow stole a piece of cheese. He flew to a _____ (1) tree with

the cheese as he thought that it would be a _____ (2) place to eat it.

A fox _____ (3) the crow and the cheese. He _____ (4) to

himself that the cheese would be delicious to eat.

With this in mind, he devised a plan to get the cheese from the crow. The fox

_____ (5) to the crow, 'You are _____ (6). I have never

before set eyes upon such a _____ (7) coat and sparkling eyes!'.

The _____ (8) was very pleased.

The fox then said to the crow, 'Since you look so magnificent I'm sure that your voice would

also be of the same quality!'.

The flattery certainly _____ (9) the crow feel very happy. In fact, it made

her want to demonstrate to the fox how _____ (10) her voice was. She

opened up her _____ (11) wide and the cheese fell to the

_____ (12). _____ (13) the fox ran towards the cheese

and picked it up.

To the crow he said, 'You may sing like an _____ (14) and look wonderful,

however, you are not _____ (15) clever!'. With that, the

fox _____ (16) away. The crow thought to herself that

next time she would not be so easily _____ (17).

Moral: Beware of flatterers. They are not to be trusted.

The Fox and the Crow

1. Show where these words can be broken between syllables; for example – him / self.

   (a) beautiful _____

   (b) devised _____

   (c) finally _____

   (d) quickly _____

   (e) shiny _____

   (f) herself _____

   (g) demonstrate _____

   (h) beware _____

   (i) magnificent _____

   (j) delicious _____

   (k) away _____

   (l) quality _____

2. Write six words which have three syllables.

   _____   _____   _____

   _____   _____   _____

3. Write a poem about the crow, following the syllable pattern in the poem below.

Fox		**Crow**
Smart fox	(2 syllables)	_____
Clever fox	(3 syllables)	_____
Quick cunning fox	(4 syllables)	_____
Crafty sneaky fox	(5 syllables)	_____

4. Crack the codes.
   Use the number and alphabet code to unjumble the message below.

A	B	C	D	E	F	G	H	I	J	K	L	M	N	O	P	Q	R	S	T	U	V	W	X	Y	Z
26	25	24	23	22	21	20	19	18	17	16	15	14	13	12	11	10	9	8	7	6	5	4	3	2	1

   (a) _____   _____   _____

        7, 19, 22   24, 9,12, 4   4, 26, 8

   _____.

       8, 7, 26, 9, 5, 18, 13, 20.

   (b) _____   _____   _____

        7,19, 22   21,12, 3   20, 12, 7

   _____   _____.

      21, 12, 12, 23   11, 12, 18, 8, 12, 13, 18, 13, 20.

The Fox and the Crow

1. Rewrite these words in the correct order to form a sentence. Punctuate the sentences.

   (a) stole crow one a cheese piece of

   _____

   _____

   (b) fox cheese a and the spied the crow

   _____

   (c) crow fox the told the beautiful was she

   _____

   (d) certainly flattery feel made happy the crow

   _____

2. Write an interesting beginning or ending for these sentences.

   (a) _____

   _____

   disappeared with the cheese.

   (b) _____

   the cheese would taste delicious.

   (c) The crow thought that next time _____

   _____

3. Unjumble the following words. Write them in a sentence.

Word	Unjumbled	Sentence
lisgpnkar		
etdtsur		
aiictngfemn		

Proverbs

A proverb is a saying that expresses a moral lesson. For example, 'Many hands make light work' (The more people helping, the easier the task).

1. Match the beginning of each proverb to its ending.

(a)	Out of sight, •	• spoil the broth.
(b)	Look before •	• twice shy.
(c)	In for a penny •	• in his mouth.
(d)	A rolling stone •	• in for a pound.
(e)	Once bitten •	• a book by its cover.
(f)	Butter wouldn't melt •	• gathers no moss.
(g)	You can't judge •	• you leap.
(h)	Too many cooks •	• out of mind.

2. Complete the following proverbs.

(a) Birds of a feather _____

(b) Six of one _____

(c) Don't count your chickens _____

(d) A friend in need _____

(e) A stitch in time _____

(f) All that glitters _____

(g) One in the hand is _____

(h) No news is _____

3. Explain the meanings of the following proverbs.

(a) The early bird catches the worm.

_____

_____

(b) Curiosity killed the cat.

_____

4. On a separate piece of paper draw your favourite proverb. Give it to a friend to solve.

Writing a Narrative

Write a narrative that has a moral to it. Here are some ideas that you could write about—stranger danger, being greedy or stealing.

Title: _____

Setting (When, who, where?)

_____

_____

_____

Initiating Event (What event starts the story?)

_____

_____

_____

Problem (What makes the story exciting?)

_____

_____

_____

Resolution (How is the problem solved?)

_____

_____

_____

Conclusion (How does the story end?)

_____

_____

_____

Edit and publish your narrative on another piece of paper. Illustrate your story.

All About Blood

A description is a framework that describes a specific living or non-living thing.
Examples of this type of writing include science reports on specific breeds of animals (e.g. German shepherds), essays, poetry, journals and medical texts.

Introduction (What is it?)

Blood is the main fluid in the body (aside from water). It has an amazing number of jobs, and no part of the body can survive without it.

An adult man has five to six litres of blood in his body, while a woman has about a litre less. A child has approximately half the amount of blood of an adult, and a four-kilogram baby has just 300 millilitres of this vital fluid.

Description
(What does it look like/is it made of?)

Blood is 55% plasma, a transparent yellowish fluid. The remainder consists of red and white blood cells and platelets. The plasma is the liquid part of the blood, while the red and white cells and the platelets are the solid part. Plasma is mostly water, but also contains proteins, sugars, waste products and other chemical elements.

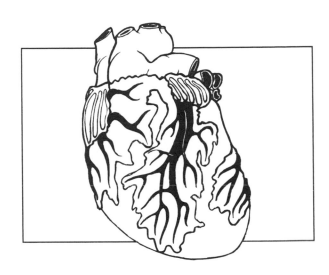

Interesting details (Special features)

The organ that pumps the blood around the body is the heart. Arteries carry blood from the heart to all parts of the body and veins return blood to the heart.

The main job of the blood is to carry oxygen and cell-building materials to every part of the body. Blood also helps to remove body wastes by carrying them to the organs that are responsible for getting rid of them or breaking them down into harmless substances. For example, the blood carries carbon dioxide (a waste) back to the lungs, where it is breathed out and replaced with oxygen. The kidneys also remove wastes. They make sure the blood does not contain poisons and that it has the right amount of water and salt in it.

Blood also carries cells that fight germs which enter the body and cause illness.

Conclusion (Ending statement)

Blood is the 'river of life' flowing through the human body. An adult who loses a litre of blood, suddenly, will faint. If a person loses too much blood, he or she will die. Blood transfusions, where 'new' blood is given to a patient, are often performed to save a person's life. For these to be successful, the 'new' blood must match the patient's blood type.

Many people's lives have been saved by blood transfusions after an accident or illness. Blood banks store the different groups of blood given by donors for use in emergencies or operations. Transfusions are also used to help people with certain illnesses, such as anaemia.

All About Blood

Use the description to answer the questions.

1. What is the main function of the blood?

   _____

   _____

2. What are the names of the solid and liquid components of the blood?

   _____

3. Which part of the body is responsible for pumping blood around the body?

   _____

4. What do the veins and arteries do? Write keywords.

Veins	Arteries

5. How is waste removed from the body?

   _____

   _____

   _____

6. When can blood transfusions take place?

   _____

   _____

7. What do you think would happen if an adult lost four litres of blood?

   _____

8. Why do you think that blood can be called the 'river of life'?

   _____

   _____

   _____

All About Blood

Blood is the main fluid in the body (aside from water). It has an amazing number of

_____(1), and no part of the body can survive without it.

An adult man has five to six litres of _____(2) in his body, while a

woman has about _____(3) litre less.

Blood is 55% _____(4), a transparent, yellowish fluid. The remainder is

consists of red and _____(5) blood cells and _____(6).

Plasma is mostly _____(7), but also contains proteins, sugars, waste

products and _____(8) chemical elements.

The organ that _____(9) the blood around the body is the heart. Arteries

carry blood from the heart to all parts of the body and the _____(10) return

blood to the heart. The main job of the blood is to _____(11)

oxygen and cell-building materials to _____(12) part of the

body. Blood also helps to remove body wastes by carrying them to the

organs that are _____(13) for getting rid of them

or breaking them down into harmless substances. Blood also

_____(14) cells that fight germs which enter the body and cause illness.

Blood is the 'river of _____'(15) flowing through the human body. An adult

who loses a _____(16) of blood, suddenly, will _____(17).

If a person loses too much blood, he or she will die. Blood transfusions, where 'new' blood is

given to a patient, are often performed to save a _____(18) life. In order

for this to be successful, the 'new' blood must _____(19) the patient's

blood type.

Many people's lives have been saved by blood _____(20) after an accident

or illness.

All About Blood

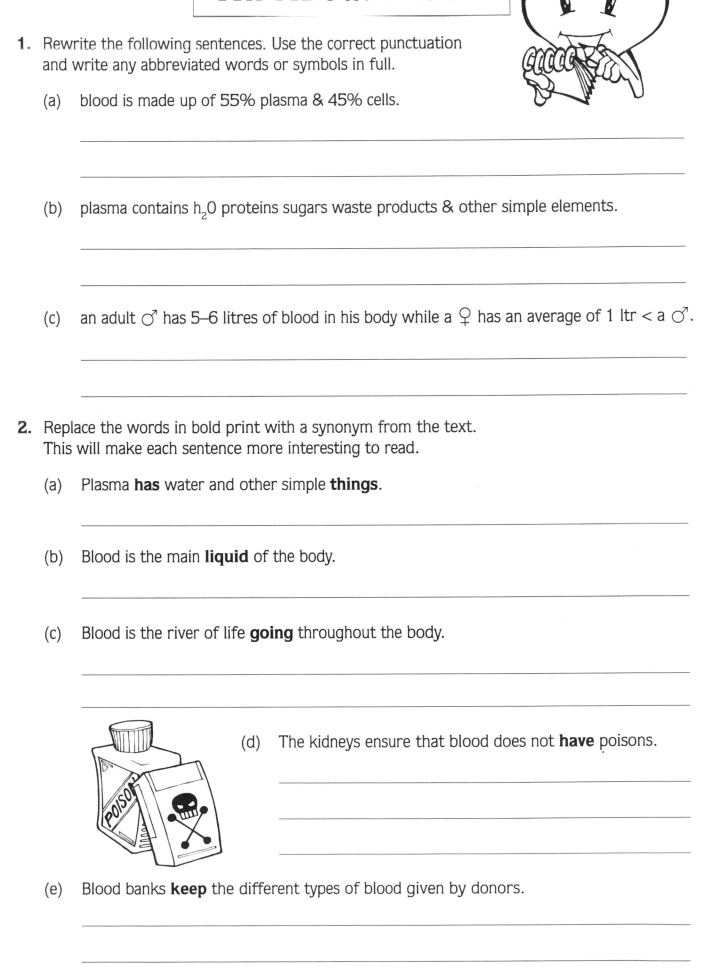

1. Rewrite the following sentences. Use the correct punctuation and write any abbreviated words or symbols in full.

    (a) blood is made up of 55% plasma & 45% cells.

    _____

    _____

    (b) plasma contains h₂0 proteins sugars waste products & other simple elements.

    _____

    _____

    (c) an adult ♂ has 5–6 litres of blood in his body while a ♀ has an average of 1 ltr < a ♂.

    _____

    _____

2. Replace the words in bold print with a synonym from the text. This will make each sentence more interesting to read.

    (a) Plasma **has** water and other simple **things**.

    _____

    (b) Blood is the main **liquid** of the body.

    _____

    (c) Blood is the river of life **going** throughout the body.

    _____

    _____

    (d) The kidneys ensure that blood does not **have** poisons.

    _____

    _____

    _____

    (e) Blood banks **keep** the different types of blood given by donors.

    _____

    _____

All About Blood

When planning our writing we need to arrange the sentences so that the facts are in the correct sequence. A paragraph begins with a topic sentence followed by related facts. Rewrite the sentences below in the correct order to form a cohesive paragraph.

1. (a) Plasma contains mostly water.

    (b) Blood is made up of 55 to 65 per cent plasma which is a transparent yellowish fluid.

    (c) The remainder is made up of red and white blood cells and platelets.

    (d) The plasma is the liquid part of the blood whereas the red and white blood cells and the platelets are the solid components.

    (e) Its other substances include proteins, sugars, waste products and other chemical elements.

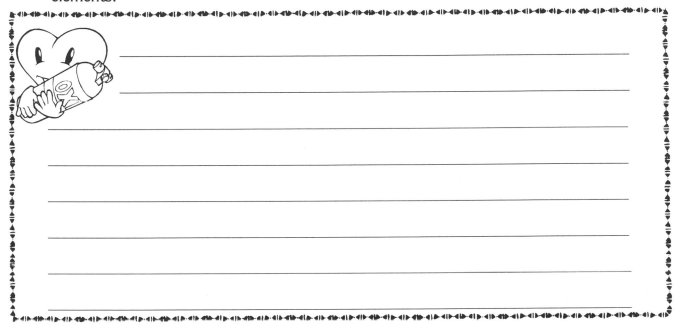

2. (a) Blood also discards waste products by carrying them to the organs that are responsible for their removal from the body or by breaking them down into harmless substances.

    (b) The primary job of blood is to carry oxygen and cell building material from the lungs around to every part of the body.

    (c) For example, the blood carries waste such as carbon dioxide back to the lungs where it is exhaled.

Writing a Description

Write a description about a body part such as the heart, lungs, skin or muscles. Use the framework below.

Title: _____

_____

Introduction (What is it?)

_____

_____

_____

_____

Description (What does it look like?)

_____

_____

_____

Interesting details (What are the important features and what do they do?)

_____

_____

_____

_____

_____

Conclusion (Ending Statement)

_____

_____

_____

_____

Edit and publish your description on another piece of paper. Illustrate your description.

Frogs

A report is a framework that describes aspects of a non-living or living thing.
It classifies them, describes their attributes, states their location and what they do.
Examples of this type of writing include science reports, newspaper articles and magazine articles.

Classification (What is it?)

Frogs are amphibians. The term 'amphibian' means having two ways of life. Frogs are both land and water dwellers.

Description (State its appearance; for example: colour, size, shape)

There are many species of frogs. They range in size from approximately 1cm to 80 cm. Frogs vary in colour. They can be brown, yellow or various shades of green and can have spots or stripes on their skin. A frog's skin is smooth and moist, allowing it to breathe.

A frog has four limbs, its hind limbs longer than its forelimbs. Its body is oblong in shape with a slight swell on its back. A frog's head comes to a rounded point at the front and has two marble-like eyes which protrude from its forehead.

Location (Where are they found?)

These unique creatures can be found all over the world from cold, wet areas to hot deserts. They can live in the water or on land. Frogs are mainly located in tropical regions where it is warm and wet. They do not like the colder temperatures but can survive varying temperatures by hibernating in lakes or damp places.

Dynamics (What does it do?)

Frogs lay clumps of eggs in water, damp soil or in special nests. The eggs hatch into tadpoles approximately one week after they are laid. These tadpoles use their strong tails to swim. They breathe through their gills. As the tadpole grows it develops forelimbs and hind limbs. Their gills disappear and lungs develop. The tadpoles then come to the surface to breathe, or survive underwater by taking oxygen from the water through their skin. Finally the tadpole loses its tail and is capable of leaving the water. These changes can take as little as three months or as long as two years. The young frogs can then take up to three years to grow to full adult size.

Frogs leap to their destination or clamber through tree branches in search of insects to eat. They use their fingers or suction pads to help them grasp twigs and climb about.

Conclusion (Ending statement)

Larger animals such as snakes and birds of prey, or mammals such as raccoons, hunt frogs. Usually they are not powerful enough to fight back. At times they may jump out of harm's way. However, camouflage is their best defence.

Frogs

Use the report to answer the questions.

1. To what type of animal does the term amphibian refer?

   _____

   _____

2. Why is it important that a frog's skin remain moist? _____

   _____

3. Where are you likely to find frogs? _____

   _____

4. List three changes that occur when a tadpole develops into a frog.

   _____

   _____

   _____

5. How long does it take for a young frog to develop into an adult?

   _____

   _____

6. What types of animals hunt frogs as their prey?

   _____

7. Why do you think frogs vary in colour?

   _____

   _____

8. In the space below, describe and illustrate the four stages of a frog's life cycle.

Frogs

Frogs are amphibians. The term _____ _____ (1) means having two ways of life.

Frogs are both land and _____ (2) dwellers.

Frogs can be brown, yellow or _____ (3) shades of green and can have spots or stripes on their skin. A frog has four limbs, its hind limbs longer than its forelimbs. Its body is oblong in shape with a slight swell on its back. A _____ (4) head comes to a rounded point at the front and has two marble-like _____ (5).

These unique creatures can be found all over the world from cold, wet areas to hot deserts. They can live in the water or on _____ (6). Frogs are mainly located in tropical regions where it is warm and _____ (7). Frogs lay clumps of eggs in water, damp soil or in special nests. The eggs _____ _____ ____ (8) into tadpoles approximately one _____ (9) after they are laid. As the tadpole grows it _____ (10) forelimbs and hind limbs. Their gills _____ (11) and lungs grow. Finally the tadpole loses its tail and is capable of leaving _____ (12) water.

Frogs leap to their destination or clamber through tree branches in search of insects to _____ (13). They use their fingers or suction pads to help them grasp twigs and climb about.

Larger animals such as snakes and birds of prey, or mammals such as raccoons, _____ (14) frogs. Usually they are not _____ (15) enough to fight back. At times they may jump out of harm's way. However, _____ (16) is their best defence.

Adjectives – 1

Adjectives are words that describe nouns. There are several different types of adjectives. Three of these are:
- Adjectives that tell us 'what kind' – **red** dress, **cold** day
- Adjectives that tell us 'how much' or 'how many' – **two** days, **some** rice
- Adjectives that tell us 'which one' – **that** girl, **each** child.

1. Write a suitable adjective for each of the nouns below.

(a) _____ skin   (b) _____ tadpoles

(c) _____ eggs   (d) _____ swamp

(e) _____ frogs   (f) _____ tree

(g) _____ desert   (h) _____ snake

2. (a) Complete these sentences by writing a suitable adjective.

(i) The _____ frog leapt over a log.

(ii) _____ tadpoles turned into frogs today.

(iii) Troy caught _____ tadpoles.

(iv) _____ frogs are coloured brown.

(v) Look at _____ tadpoles in the pond!

(vi) A frog's skin is _____ and moist.

(b) Write the adjectives above in the correct box.

tells 'what kind'	tells 'how much/many'	tells 'which one'

3. Write a synonym and antonym for these adjectives.

Adjective	Synonym	Antonym
(a) **large** frog		
(b) **strong** tails		
(c) **damp** places		

Adjectives – 2

Adjectives can be in a comparative form (comparing two things) or superlative form (comparing three or more things).

For example:

A big frog.   (base)
A bigger frog.   (comparative)
The biggest frog.   (superlative)

Sometimes the word 'more' is used for the comparative form and the word 'most' is used for the superlative form.

For example:
colourful, more colourful, most colourful.

1. Complete the table below using the comparative and superlative forms of each base word.

Base	Comparative	Superlative
smooth		
special		
powerful		
young		
little		
slimy		

2. Use the correct form of the word 'lovely' to complete the sentences.

   (a)   It was the _____ bouquet of flowers I'd seen.

   (b)   The roses were _____ than the tulips.

   (c)   Andrew was given a _____ outfit for his first birthday.

   (d)   The _____ dress in the shop was in the sale.

3. Use the base words below to write a nonsense paragraph about frogs. You can also use the comparative or superlative form of each adjective.

   • green   • beautiful   • small   • strong   • slimy

   _____

   _____

   _____

   _____

Writing a Report

Write a report on an animal of your choice. Follow the framework below.

Title: _____

Classification:

_____

_____

_____

_____

Description:

_____

_____

_____

_____

Location:

_____

_____

_____

_____

Dynamics:

_____

_____

_____

_____

Conclusion (Ending of statement)

_____

_____

_____

_____

Edit and publish your report on another piece of paper. Illustrate your report.

Sultana and Apricot Rock Cakes

A procedure is a framework that outlines how something is done. It is sequential and follows steps.

Examples of this type of writing include recipes, experiments and instruction manuals.

Topic: Food

Goal: To make Sultana and Apricot Rock Cakes

Requirements:

Ingredients:
$\frac{1}{3}$ cup of milk
2 cups of self-raising flour
3 tablespoons of sultanas
$\frac{1}{4}$ cup of sugar
$\frac{1}{4}$ teaspoon of cinnamon
$\frac{1}{2}$ cup of chopped dried apricots
90 g melted butter
1 egg
2 tablespoons of honey
extra butter

Utensils:
measuring cups
tablespoon
baking tray
mixing spoon
sieve
large bowl
greased paper

Method:

1. Lightly grease a baking tray with the extra butter.

2. Sieve the flour, sugar and cinnamon into a bowl.

3. Stir thoroughly.

4. Add the melted butter, egg and honey into the mixture.

5. Slowly add the milk. Add the sultanas and apricots and mix well.

6. Place tablespoons of the mixture onto the baking tray.

7. Bake in a moderate (180º) oven for 20 minutes.

8. Remove from tray and leave to cool.

Evaluation:

Taste a Sultana and Apricot Rock Cake.

Makes about 15.

Sultana and Apricot Rock Cakes

Use the procedure to answer the questions.

1. Write a beginning or ending for each sentence below about the recipe.

    (a)   Add the egg and honey _____.

    (b)   _____ for 20 minutes.

    (c)   Lightly grease a baking tray _____.

    (d)   _____ onto the baking tray.

    (e)   Sieve the flour, sugar _____.

    (f)   _____

          _____ and mix well.

2. Rewrite the sentences above in the correct order.

3. Rewrite the correct amounts needed for these ingredients.

    (a) [1/3 cup] 3 cups of milk   (b) [   ] 2 tablespoons of sultanas

    (c) [   ] 1/4 g sugar   (d) [   ] 4 teaspoons of cinnamon

    (e) [   ] 9 g butter   (f) [   ] 2 cups chopped apricots

    (g) [   ] 3 eggs   (h) [   ] 2 teaspoons of honey

Sultana and Apricot Rock Cakes

Topic: Food

Goal: To make Sultana and _____ (1) Rock Cakes

Requirements: _____ .(2)

$\frac{1}{3}$ cup of milk

2 _____ (3) of self-raising flour

3 tablespoons of sultanas

$\frac{1}{4}$ cup of sugar

$\frac{1}{4}$ teaspoon of cinnamon

$\frac{1}{2}$ cup of _____ (4) dried apricots

90 g butter

1 egg

2 tablespoons of honey

_____ (5) melted butter

Utensils:

measuring cups

tablespoon

baking tray

_____ (6) spoon

sieve

large bowl

greased _____ (7)

Method:

1. _____ (8) grease a baking tray with the extra butter.

2. Sieve the flour, sugar and _____ (9) into a bowl.

3. _____ (10) thoroughly.

4. Add the egg and honey into the mixture.

5. Slowly add the milk. Add the sultanas and apricots and

   _____ (11) well.

6. Place tablespoons of the mixture onto the baking tray.

7. Bake in a _____ (12) (180°) oven for 20 minutes.

8. _____ (13) from tray and leave to cool.

Evaluation: Taste a Sultana and Apricot Rock Cake. Makes _____ (14) 15.

Verbs

Verbs are action words. All sentences contain at least one verb.

1. Complete these sentences using verbs.

   (a)   The mixture must be _____ thoroughly.

   (b)   _____ in a moderate oven for 20 minutes.

   (c)   Knives can be used to _____, _____ and

   _____ food.

   (d)   Remember to _____ up your mess after

   _____.

2. Unjumble the verbs in bold in these sentences.

   (a)   Chloe **ttsead** _____ the rock cakes

   they had **docoek** _____.

   (b)   **rBake** _____ the eggs carefully and

   alpce _____ them in a bowl.

   (c)   Ensure the ingredients are **eixmd** _____ well.

   (d)   **esuMaer** _____ the ingredients correctly before **dndiag**

   _____ them to the mixture.

3. Unjumble the following verbs. Write each one in a sentence.

Word	Unjumbled	Sentence
koconig		
msureaing		
ppecohd		

Writing a Procedure

Look in magazines and cookbooks to help you find a treat that you would like to make.
Write up the procedure below.

Topic: _____

Goal: _____

_____

Requirements:

Ingredients: _____

_____

_____

_____

Utensils: _____

_____

_____

Method: _____

_____

_____

_____

_____

_____

Evaluation: _____

_____

_____

Draw pictures to show how you made your treat.

Edit and publish your procedure on another piece of paper.

How the Ear Works

An explanation is a framework that outlines how something works or is made. It gives a definition, describes the components, how it operates, and states where it can be applied.

Examples of this type of writing include health and science writing, essays and handbooks.

Definition (What is it?)

The ear is the organ of hearing and of balance. The ear's main functions are to hear and to aid with balance.

Components/Parts (Describe the parts)

The ear is divided into three main sections: the outer ear, the middle ear and the inner ear. The outer ear consists of the external part of the ear (sometimes called the flap or pinna), the auditory canal and the eardrum. The middle ear consists of three small bones known as the hammer, anvil and stirrup and the inner ear consists of tubes and sacs filled with fluid.

Operations (How it works)

The outer ear is responsible for collecting the soundwaves and directing them through the auditory canal to the eardrum. When these soundwaves reach the eardrum, the eardrum experiences movement and transmits vibrations. These vibrations are communicated to three small bones in the middle ear and then to the fluid in the inner ear, which also begins to vibrate. The vibrations result in messages being transmitted via a nerve (auditory nerve) to the brain and sound is heard.

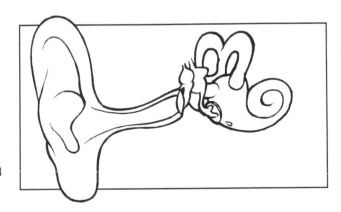

The ear is also important for balance. Our balance depends on detectors in the inner ear, which send messages to the brain. As a result of this, messages are sent to muscles around the body which help to maintain our balance.

Applications (When and where it works or is applied)

When you hear a sound of any sort such as talking, singing, barking and chirping you know that your ears have been hard at work. The fact that we can walk in a straight line or run inside the lines on a racetrack is due to our ears providing us with balance.

Some people's ears don't work as well as others and they may require hearing aids. Unfortunately, there is a percentage of the population who are deaf and, therefore, cannot hear at all. Fortunately, technology to assist the deaf to hear is improving all the time.

Conclusion (Ending comment/special features)

Although we are not consciously aware of it, our ears are constantly working. They never turn off or have a break! They are amazing organs.

How the Ear Works

Use the explanation to answer the questions.

1. The ear has two important functions. Name them.

    (i) _____

    (ii) _____

2. What are the names of the major ear sections?

    _____

    _____

    _____

3. Name the nerve that carries messages from the ear to the brain.

    _____

4. Finish labelling the diagram of the ear correctly.

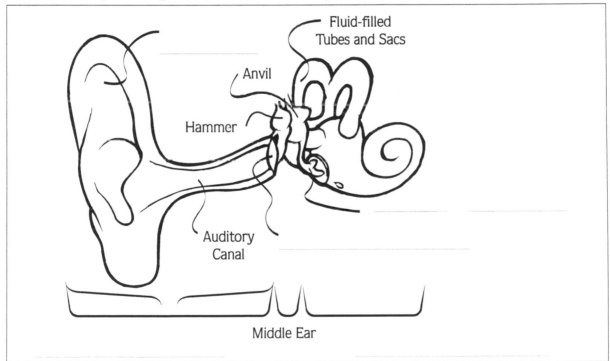

Fluid-filled Tubes and Sacs

Anvil

Hammer

Auditory Canal

Middle Ear

5. Why is the ear an amazing organ?

    _____

    _____

6. How do you think you could receive messages if you were deaf?

    _____

How the Ear Works

The ear is the organ of hearing. It is also the organ of _____(1).

The ear is divided into three main sections: the outer ear, the middle ear and the

_____(2) ear. The outer ear consists of the external part of the ear, the

auditory canal and the eardrum. The middle ear _____(3) of three small

bones known as the hammer, anvil and stirrup and the inner _____(4)

consists of tubes and sacs filled with fluid.

The outer ear is responsible for collecting the soundwaves and directing

_____(5) through the auditory canal to the eardrum.

When these soundwaves reach the eardrum, the eardrum experiences movement and

transmits _____(6). These vibrations are _____(7) to

three small bones in the middle ear and then to the fluid in the inner ear, which also

begins to _____(8). The vibrations result in messages being transmitted via

a nerve to the brain and _____(9) is heard.

The ear is also important for balance. Our balance depends on detectors in the

_____(10) ear, which send messages to the _____(11).

As a result of this, messages are sent to muscles around the body which

_____(12) to maintain our balance.

When you hear a sound you know that your ears have been hard at

_____(13) and the fact that we can walk in a straight

line or _____(14) inside the lines on a racetrack is

all thanks to our ears.

Although we are not consciously aware of it, our ears are constantly

_____(15). They never turn off or have a break!

They are _____(16) organs.

Compound Words

Compound words are made by joining two separate words. For example, head + ache = headache.

1. Unjumble the words below and join to make compound words.

Hint: They all begin with 'ear':

(a) rae   +   mrdu   =   _____

(b) are   +   bole   =   _____

(c) era   +   rgni   =   _____

2. Many parts of the body are also compound words. Match the words in the first column with those in the second column to make compound words.

(a) fore •   • pit   _____

(b) arm •   • cage   _____

(c) knee •   • lash   _____

(d) collar •   • nail   _____

(e) eye •   • head   _____

(f) finger •   • cap   _____

(g) rib •   • bone   _____

3. Write a body part to make a compound word.

(a) _____ ball   (b) _____ brush

(c) _____ pick   (d) _____ ache

(e) _____ band   (f) _____ beat

4. Complete the sentences using compound words.

(a) Be careful not to burst your _____ when diving into deep water.

(b) Ingrown _____ can be very painful.

(c) Your lungs are situated behind your _____ .

(d) After completing the marathon his _____ rose significantly.

Writing an Explanation

Choose a body organ and write an explanation about how it works; for example – heart, eye or lungs. Follow the framework below.

Title: _____

Definition (What is it?)

_____

_____

Components/Parts (Describe the parts)

_____

_____

_____

_____

Operations (How it works)

_____

_____

_____

_____

Applications (When and where it works or is applied)

_____

_____

_____

_____

Conclusion (Ending comment/special feature)

_____

_____

_____

_____

Edit and publish your explanation on another piece of paper.

School Uniforms

An exposition is a framework that evaluates an issue. Arguments both for and against the topic are given to persuade the audience.
Examples of this type of writing include debates, speeches and critical reviews and policies.

Introduction (Define the topic)

Most schools encourage pupils to wear a school uniform. There are a variety of reasons why schools promote the wearing of uniforms.

Arguments for: (Ideas that support the topic)

School uniforms enhance your appearance by helping to make you appear neat and tidy. People often comment about how smart uniforms look.

Safety is an important issue. School uniforms are also designed to protect you. Blazers and jumpers are worn to protect you from the cold. Sturdy footwear protects you from dangerous objects such as broken glass.

The wearing of a uniform also encourages school pride and a sense of unity among pupils. When you wear a uniform outside the school grounds people can identify which school you come from.

The cost of a uniform is another factor to consider. The price is the same for everyone and it would often be cheaper than having to buy a variety of clothes.

Arguments against: (Ideas that oppose the topic)

Pupils should be able to select their own clothes to wear to school. This allows for individuals to express their identity.

The design and colour of a uniform could be unflattering to some individuals. Some pupils find certain items of a uniform uncomfortable to wear, such as a tie or heavy blazer.

Conclusion: (Ending comment)

However, while individual choice is important, we cannot overlook the positive aspects of wearing a uniform—appearance, safety and group unity, which may be of greater importance.

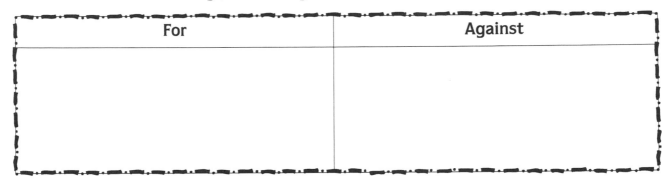

School Uniforms

Use the exposition to answer the questions.

1. Write two reasons for and against wearing a uniform.

For	Against

2. How could a school uniform protect you?

_____

_____

3. How do you think wearing a school uniform encourages school pride?

_____

_____

_____

4. Write a definition for the following words:

    (a) presentable – _____

    (b) uniform – _____

    (c) expensive – _____

5. Do you think pupils should wear a uniform? Why/Why not?

_____

_____

6. The police wear uniforms. Name four other occupations that have uniforms.

(i) _____ (ii) _____

(iii) _____ (iv) _____

7. On a separate piece of paper, design an entire school uniform (hat, footwear, shirt, trousers etc). Don't forget to include an emblem and colours.

School Uniforms

Most schools encourage pupils to wear a school uniform. There are a

_____(1) of reasons why schools promote the wearing

of _____(2).

School uniforms enhance your _____(3) by helping to make you appear

_____(4) and tidy. People often comment about how smart school uniforms

_____(5).

Safety is an important issue. School uniforms are also _____(6) to protect

you. Blazers and jumpers are worn to _____(7) you from the cold.

Sturdy footwear protects you from dangerous objects such as broken

_____(8).

The wearing of a uniform also _____(9) school pride and a sense of unity

among pupils. When you wear a _____(10) outside the school grounds

people can identify which school you come from.

The cost of a uniform is another important fact to _____(11).

The _____(12) is the same for everyone and it would often be cheaper than

having to buy a variety of clothes.

Pupils should be able to select their own clothes to wear to school. This

allows for _____(13) to express their identity.

Others say that the design and colour of a _____(14)

could be unflattering to some individuals.

However, while individual choice is important, we cannot

overlook the positive aspects of wearing a uniform—appearance, safety and group unity,

which may be of greater _____(15).

Planning an Exposition

It is important to plan your exposition writing.
Here is a topic for you to plan.

'Should the school canteen sell sweets?'

With a partner, write reasons why the canteen should sell sweets and then reasons why the canteen should not sell sweets. Complete this activity on the planning framework provided on page 40.

Arguments For	Arguments Against

Writing an Exposition:

Now that you have listed reasons for and against the topic write what you believe and the reasons why.

I think _____

_____

_____

because _____

_____

_____

_____

Writing an Exposition

Write your own exposition using the framework below.

Title: _____

_____

Introduction (Define topic):

_____
_____
_____
_____

Arguments for (Ideas that support the topic):

_____
_____
_____
_____

Arguments against (Ideas that don't agree with the topic):

_____
_____
_____
_____

Conclusion (Ending comment):

_____
_____
_____
_____

Edit and publish your writing on another piece of paper.

Learning Centre

These activities can be photocopied, enlarged to A3 and made into individual activity cards. Standard equipment required are scissors, card, glue, paper, pencils and felt pens.

 1

Write a procedure explaining how to make a stained glass window.

2

Imagine you are working on a cruise ship. Write a diary entry. Include, the date, 'Dear Diary' and then retell the events of a typical day. Follow the recount framework.

3

Are your school rules appropriate? Write an exposition explaining what you think.

4

Write a description of a spider. Include a labelled illustration.

 5

Write a report about a minibeast. Include a labelled illustration.

6

Write a narrative retelling either your favourite fable or fairytale.

7

Design your dream home. Label each room and special features.

8

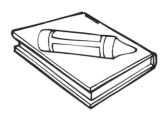

Design a cover for your latest book. Don't forget to include the author and illustrator.

 9

Make a colouring book of animals. Write a short paragraph under each heading describing each animal's features.

 10

Write a book report on your favourite book. Tell us what the book is about, your favourite part and why you liked it.

Learning Centre

11 Read the limerick below. Try writing your own by following the pattern. Illustrate it.

There once was a man from Peru
Who dreamt he was eating his shoe
When he woke in the night
He sat up in fright
And found it was perfectly true.

12

Design and make a card for a friend.

13

Write a list of your hobbies. Include an illustration.

14

Draw and label a map of your school.

15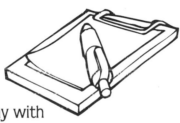

Make up a play with a friend. Act it out.

16

Make up as many rhyming poems as you can. Illustrate them.

17

List 10 reasons why you should be selected for a mission to the moon.

18

Write a procedure explaining how to make a cake.

19 Think of as many riddles as you can. Write them down and then give them to a friend to answer.

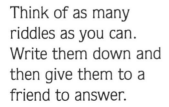

20

Use this sentence starter to write a narrative story: 'If I won a million pounds ...'

Learning Centre Evaluation

Name _____

| Activity no. |

What task did I complete?

_____

What I enjoyed the most:

_____

_____

What I learnt from the activity:

_____

_____

What was the most challenging part of the task?

| Score |
| **/10** |

_____

_____

Learning Centre Evaluation

Name _____

| Activity no. |

What task did I complete?

_____

What I enjoyed the most:

_____

What I learnt from the activity:

_____

What was the most challenging part of the task?

| Score |
| **/10** |

_____

Answers

The World Cup Football Finals

Page 2
1. They were going to watch football.
2. The weather conditions changed.
3. Afternoon—because they took lunch to the game.
4. The final stage of the game because the score was equal.
5. The teams had excellent teamwork and skills.
6. Yes. He congratulated the other team in an honourable manner.

7–8. Teacher check

Page 3
1. wind's   2. weather   3. buddy   4. team   5. was
6. clouds   7. lunch   8. bursting   9. tension   10. but
11. and   12. final   13. extra   14. Italy   15. their
16. loss   17. team   18. sport

Page 4
1. lucky, unlucky; dull, bright; enemy, buddy; strong, weak; commenced, ceased; happy, miserable; exciting, boring; won, lost
2. results, score; more, extra; strong, tough; wonderful, great; witness, see; staring, looking; stopped, ceased; fortunately, luckily
3. Teacher check

Page 5
1. (a) game, miserable, Saturday, tickets, weather
   (b) barracked, brightly, buddy, ceased, decided
   (c) captain, clambered, equal, honourable, Italy
   (d) wind, window, witnessed, won, world
2. (a) feet   (b) packed   (c) dad

3–4. Teacher check

The Fox and the Crow

Page 8
1–2. Teacher check
3. devised – planned; flattery – excessive praise
4. The fox used flattery to get the crow to open her mouth by showing off her voice.
5. Teacher check
6. Foolish
7. Always be on your guard
8. Teacher check

Page 9
1. nearby   2. great   3. spied   4. thought
5. said   6. beautiful   7. shiny   8. crow
9. made   10. magnificent   11. mouth   12. ground
13. Quickly   14. angel   15. very   16. ran
17. fooled

Page 10
1. (a) beau/ti/ful (b) de/vised (c) fi/nal/ly (d) quick/ly
   (e) shi/ny (f) her/self (g) de/mon/strate (h) be/ware
   (i) mag/nif/i/cent (j) del/i/cious (k) a/way (l) qual/i/ty

2–3. Teacher check
4. (a) The crow was starving.
   (b) The fox got food poisoning.

Page 11
1. (a) A crow stole one piece of cheese.

(b) A fox spied the crow and the cheese.
   (c) The fox told the crow she was beautiful.
   (d) Flattery certainly made the crow feel happy.
2. Teacher check
3. sparkling, trusted, magnificent

Page 12
1. (a) Out of sight, out of mind.   (b) Look before you leap.
   (c) In for a penny, in for a pound.
   (d) A rolling stone gathers no moss.
   (e) Once bitten, twice shy.
   (f) Butter wouldn't melt in his mouth.
   (g) You can't judge a book by its cover.
   (h) Too many cooks spoil the broth.
2. (a) Birds of a feather flock together.
   (b) Six of one, half a dozen of the other.
   (c) Don't count your chickens before they hatch.
   (d) A friend in need is a friend indeed.
   (e) A stitch in time saves nine.
   (f) All that glitters is not gold.
   (g) One in the hand is worth two in the bush.
   (h) No news is good news.
3. (a) The earlier you begin, the greater your chance of success.
   (b) Inquisitiveness can get you into trouble.

All About Blood

Page 15
1. To carry oxygen and cell building material to every part of the body.
2. Plasma, white and red blood cells and platelets.
3. The heart.
4. Veins return blood from the heart to all parts of the body.
   Arteries carry blood to the heart.
5. The blood carries them to organs that get rid of them or break them down into harmless substances.
6. Emergencies, accidents or illness.
7. They would probably die.
8. It is necessary for survival.

Page 16
1. jobs   2. blood   3. one   4. plasma   5. white
6. platelets 7. water   8. other   9. pumps   10. veins
11. carry   12. every   13. responsible   14. carries
15. life   16. litre   17. faint   18. person's
19. match 20. transfusions

Page 17
1. (a) Blood is made up of fifty five percent plasma and forty five percent cells.
   (b) Plasma contains water, proteins, sugars, waste products and other simple elements.
   (c) An adult male has five to six litres of blood in his body while a female has an average of one litre less than a male.
2. (a) contains, substances (b) fluid (c) flowing
   (d) contain (e) store

Page 18
1. (b), (c), (d), (a), (e)   2. (b), (a), (c)

Frogs

Page 21
1. Frogs. They are both land and water dwellers.
2. To allow it to breathe.
3. Cold, wet areas and hot deserts, in land or in water.
4. It develops forelimbs, hind limbs and lungs.
5. Up to three years.
6. Snakes, birds and raccoons.
7. Camouflage
8. Teacher check

Page 22
1. amphibian 2. water 3. various 4. frog's
5. eyes 6. land 7. wet 8. hatch
9. week 10. develops 11. disappear 12. the
13. eat 14. hunt 15. powerful 16. camouflage

Page 23
1–3. Teacher check

Page 24
1.

Base	Comparative	Superlative
smooth	smoother	smoothest
special	more special	most special
powerful	more powerful	most powerful
young	younger	youngest
little	littler	littlest
slimy	slimier	slimiest

2. (a) loveliest (b) lovelier (c) lovely (d) loveliest
3. Teacher check

Sultana and Apricot Rock Cakes

Page 27
1. (a) Add the egg and honey into the mixture.
   (b) Bake in a moderate (180°) oven for 20 minutes.
   (c) Lightly grease a baking tray with the extra butter.
   (d) Place tablespoons of the mixture onto the baking tray.
   (e) Sieve the flour, sugar and cinnamon into a bowl.
   (f) Add the sultanas and apricots and mix well.
2. (c) (e) (a) (f) (d) (b)
3. (a) $\frac{1}{3}$ cup of milk (b) 3 tablespoons of sultanas
   (c) $\frac{1}{4}$ cup of sugar
   (d) $\frac{1}{4}$ teaspoon of cinnamon (e) 90 g butter
   (f) $\frac{1}{2}$ cup chopped dried apricots (g) 1 egg
   (h) 2 tablespoons of honey

Page 28
1. Apricot 2. Ingredients 3. cups 4. chopped
5. extra 6. mixing 7. paper 8. Lightly
9. cinnamon 10. Stir 11. mix
12. moderate 13. Remove 14. about

Page 29
1. Teacher check
2. (a) tasted, cooked (b) Break, place (c) mixed
   (d) Measure, adding
3. cooking, measuring, chopped

Page 32
1. hearing, balance
2. The outer, middle and inner ear.
3. Auditory nerve

4.

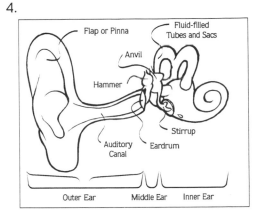

5. It is constantly working on hearing and balancing.
6. Hearing aid, sign language.

Page 33
1. balance 2. inner 3. consists 4. ear
5. them 6. vibrations 7. communicated
8. vibrate 9. sound 10. inner 11. brain
12. help 13. work 14. run 15. working
16. amazing

Page 34
1. (a) eardrum (b) earlobe (c) earring
2. (a) forehead (b) armpit (c) kneecap (d) collarbone
   (e) eyelash (f) fingernail (g) ribcage
3. Teacher check
4. (a) eardrum (b) toenails (c) ribcage (d) heartbeat

School Uniforms

Page 37
1–7 Teacher check

Page 38
1. variety 2. uniforms 3. appearance 4. neat
5. look 6. designed 7. protect 8. glass
9. encourages 10. uniform 11. consider 12. price
13. individuals 14. uniform 15. importance